Goat Chinese Horoscope 2025

By

IChingHunFùyǒu FengShuisu

Table of Contents

Introduce

The character of people born in the year of the GOAT

People born in this year enjoy romance, fantasies, fantasies, and art, are constantly in need of love and protection, are afraid of failure, and prefer to look at the world first. People born in this year are extremely lazy. So you prefer to associate with wealthy people, dislike people of lower social standing, and prefer convenience. Because people born in this year do not dare to make a decisive decision and do not dare to do anything unless they are confident, they must carefully consider what they will do before doing it. This year's births are unregulated. Not suitable for business, craftsman, artist, or writer, or a career that requires creativity and artistic abilities. This year's babies are romantic. Everyone is drawn to the charm because it is sensitive, gentle, and affectionate.

Strength:
When you are given the last assignment, you will do your absolute best.

Weaknesses:
You tend to regret it aloud, no matter how minor.

Love:
People born in this year are frequently successful in love and outstanding at work. Finance and love are especially fond of fantasies about love going far in particular, love someone who likes someone who is always passionate about it. When you care deeply about someone, you will give your all. You are completely disappointed when you are disappointed. People born this year, on the other hand, are not afraid of love so easily that they can be duped repeatedly. It takes a long time for people born in this year to find their soul mate, and once they do, their love life is often long.

Suitable Career:

Jobs that help people are ideal for those born in the Year of the Goat. They can be social services such as doctors, nurses, restaurants, hotels, handicrafts, arts and crafts, agriculture, or the sale of construction equipment. Construction contractors, engineers, designers, real estate workers, real estate agents, public relations officers, company employees, clerks, secretaries, lawyers, artists, singers, and actors, among other occupations, are all suitable for those born in the Year the Goat.

Year of the GOAT (Wood) | (1943) & (2003)

"Goats in a herd" a person born in the year of the GOAT at the age of 82 years (1943) and 22 years (2003)

Overview

For seniors in this age group, this year you must take good care of your health, especially during the 12th Chinese month (January 5 - February 2), the 2nd Chinese month (March 5 - April 3), the 3rd Chinese month (April 4 - May 4), and the 5th Chinese month (June 5 - July 6). Be careful of illnesses. You should find time to pay homage to the Tiger God Shrine, which will help alleviate the disaster. Do not interfere or be fussy with your children's matters. Also, be careful of danger and mourning. If you have the opportunity, you should find time to make merit, donate, and save animals. This will help you feel calmer and happier. You should be cheerful and let go of problems for your physical and mental health.

For young men and women aged 22, this year you should think carefully before doing any activities. You should communicate clearly so that the work that comes out will not be wrong. In terms of education, you have the opportunity to study both domestically and internationally. If the scholarship application has a fair contract, you should not miss the opportunity. For those who are entering the workforce, being humble, constantly developing yourself, and developing new and up-to-date skills will help you cope with changes and pave the way for a bright future. There are good opportunities for applying for a government job or starting your own business. However, due to the group of bad stars that are orbiting and focusing on your zodiac sign, it will cause accidents and unexpected current expenses that will cause you to lack liquidity. This year, you should plan your spending carefully because if you spend carelessly, you may face a drought. If you have to escape to borrow money from the informal sector, it will cause you even more trouble. Starting a new job investing in stocks or investing in various fields this year, there is a high chance of being cheated. You must be careful or you may face a loss of property.

Career and Business

This year, if you choose to continue your studies, it is a good opportunity. Therefore, you should strive hard and study hard to complete your studies. Gain experience along the way as a supplement. This will help you have a bright future. If you choose to work or do your own business, this is the first step to come out and experience the outside world. Please study hard from your seniors or adults. Do not be biased. This will be beneficial to you later. In your work, you should build good relationships with both your supervisor and colleagues. This will help you have a smooth career. The months when your work or studies will be hindered and have problems are the 12th Chinese month (January 5 - February 2), the 2nd Chinese month (March 5 - April 3), the 3rd Chinese month (April 4 - May 4), and the 5th Chinese month (June 5 - July 6), when you cannot be impatient at work or mistakes will happen. When signing any contracts during this period, you should carefully check the details to avoid problems later. In addition, you should not invest in anything new or more because you may be cheated. The months when your work or study will have a bright direction are the 6th Chinese month (July 7 - August 6), the 7th Chinese month (August 7 - September 6), the 9th Chinese month (October 8 - November 6), and the 10th Chinese month (November 7 - December 6). For some work or investment matters, you can consult with teachers or elders in the house. This will help reduce wrong decisions and prevent the loss of money in investments.

Financial

The fortune of the person's financial luck fluctuates greatly. Although this year there will be some money from windfalls, if you are greedy, you may be in the red. Therefore, financial planning is necessary. You should take good care of the liquidity of your money in your pocket so that you do not encounter any problems. You should also avoid doing any kind of illegal business. Otherwise, you will be involved in trouble. Especially during the 12th Chinese month (January 5 - February 2), the 2nd Chinese month (March 5 - April 3), the 3rd Chinese month (April 4 - May 4), and the 5th Chinese month (June 5 - July 6), when you are prohibited from lending money to anyone or being a guarantor. You should refrain from gambling and taking risks. You must also be careful of scammers.

You must also be careful of unexpected large expenses that will cause a lack of liquidity. The months when your finances flow smoothly are the 6th Chinese month (7 July – 6 August), the 7th Chinese month (7 August – 6 September), the 9th Chinese month (8 October – 6 November), and the 10th Chinese month (7 November – 6 December).

Family

This year, events within your family will be a mix of good and bad. The good part is that you will meet a patron for help. The bad part will be a result of evil stars, which will cause accidents, as well as impact the health and safety of the elderly and family members. You may also experience mourning for an elderly relative, especially during the months when there will be problems and chaos within the family, which are the 12th Chinese month (January 5 – February 2), the 2nd Chinese month (March 5 – April 3), the 3rd Chinese month (April 4 – May 4), and the 5th Chinese month (June 5 – July 6). Be careful of arguing with people in the family. Also, be careful of damage to valuables, loss, and danger from criminals. This year, relatives are in good shape. Overall, you will meet good friends who will give you advice about work, suggest ways to make a living, and help you with things you are not good at. However, be careful of friends who wish you ill, some of whom have ulterior motives and will expose your bad things.

Love

The first six months of the year are sweet and sweet. Even vegetable soup is sweet. After the middle of the year and the second six months, everything feels irritating. To make matters worse, temporary love is more charming. You must control yourself, use your mind, and know how to distinguish. You must take responsibility for each person's love. In particular, the months when your love will easily encounter problems and arguments are the 12th Chinese month (January 5 - February 2), the 2nd Chinese month (March 5 - April 3), the 3rd Chinese month (April 4 - May 4), and the 5th Chinese month (June 5 - July 6). You should be careful with your words and avoid trains. Don't let them run into each other. If you like someone or have feelings for someone, you should give time to one person. Don't manage to be close to many people at once. Some people can't stand it. If you don't have feelings for them, you shouldn't give them a chance because it will cause misunderstandings and arguments. You should also avoid going to entertainment venues that may bring back diseases.

Health

The health of both people in this age group is not good. Be careful of illness and body aches, which will cause high medical expenses. In addition, there is a chance of mourning for an elder relative, so do not be careless. For the elderly, be careful of tripping and falling when walking. When traveling outside the home, you should have someone accompany you.

Take your medicine as prescribed by the doctor and do light exercise. For young people, this year you should be careful of accidents and bleeding.

Especially during the months when you should take care of your health closely, which are the 12th Chinese month (January 5 - February 2), the 2nd Chinese month (March 5 - April 3), the 3rd Chinese month (April 4 - May 4), and the 5th Chinese month (June 5 - July 6). Be extra careful when working with machinery or using metal equipment. Do not be careless when using the road. You must take care of your hygiene. Drinking, and consuming intoxicants, alcohol, and e-cigarettes will damage your health. If you can quit, it will be very good.

Year of the GOAT (Golden) | (1955) & (2015)

"The Mighty Goat " is a person born in the year of the GOAT at the age of 70 years (1955) and 10 years (2015)

Overview

For senior horoscope people in this age group, this year, due to the influence of the evil star group, you will be involved in a chaotic mess. Therefore, in every job, you should look carefully before doing it. Today, you need to find an heir to take over the work to ease the burden. You cannot be impatient with every activity. Even though you have a lot of experience, your body cannot do it immediately when your heart tells you to. Therefore, having an heir or assistant to take over, along with your experience in analyzing various matters, will still progress. However, the important thing this year is the health problem. Because the horoscope house is hit by two evil stars, it often directly affects unexpected events, the chaos that makes the family lack peace, accidents, and illnesses that will ensue. Be careful of gastritis, joint pain, headaches, and high blood pressure. Therefore, if you have any abnormal symptoms, see a doctor immediately, control your diet, and find time to exercise lightly. Do not be stressed and you will be at ease.

For the young people in the Year of the Goat, the influence of the stars makes this year not so smooth. In terms of studying, you should be more diligent than before. In terms of playing, parents should not overlook safety. They should always warn children to be careful in doing various activities, including traveling and not being careless. Beware of unexpected events. Beware of bloodshed from accidents.

Career and Business

On the career path, although it moves slowly, overall there is still progress. What you should pay attention to is not to be hasty in making big decisions and to see clearly before doing so, especially the matters that are bound by contracts. Also, in human resource management, transfer of positions, etc., you must be careful of conflicts, especially the months that are not supportive for you are the 12th Chinese month (January 5 - February 2), the 2nd Chinese month (March 5 - April 3), the 3rd Chinese month (April 4 - May 4), and the 5th Chinese month (June 5 - July 6). During the aforementioned months, your work will encounter obstacles. Be careful of protests among people in the organization. Be careful not to deliver work on time because interference will cause damage. There is a chance that you will be cheated when making a contract or being hired. Be more careful when checking the contract. Also, you should not expand your investment because there is a chance that you will be cheated. The months when your work and investments are bright and prosperous are the 6th Chinese month (7 July - 6 August), the 7th Chinese month (7 August - 6 September), the 9th Chinese month (8 October - 6 November), and the 10th Chinese month (7 November - 6 December). This is another time suitable for finding an heir to continue the work help look after investments or take care of the business, all of which will create good returns.

Financial

The fortune of the person is considered moderate. Although there is some fortune, if you are greedy and spend heavily, it may be damaged. This year, you should save money, not be extravagant, and plan your finances carefully so that you will not encounter problems later. Especially during the months when your finances will be stuck and unexpected expenses will occur, namely, the 12th Chinese month (January 5 - February 2), the 2nd Chinese month (March 5 - April 3), the 3rd Chinese month (April 4 - May 4), and the 5th Chinese month (June 5 - July 6). Do not gamble, do not lend money or sign financial guarantees, and do not invest in illegal businesses. Be careful of investing or you will fall victim to fraud. The months when your finances will flow smoothly are the 6th Chinese month (July 7 – August 6), the 7th Chinese month (August 7 – September 6), the 9th Chinese month (October 8 – November 6), and the 10th Chinese month (November 7 – December 6).

Family

Even though this year there may be good news and auspicious events happening in the house, there is still the influence of the evil stars that are disturbing, which often cause arguments and conflicts among the people in the house, resulting in a lack of peace in the family, especially accidents and health problems of the family members. Family members may be deceived or enticed to get involved in legal cases, causing trouble. Also, be careful of mourning for the elders, especially during the months when the family will have problems and chaos, which are the 12th Chinese month (January 5 - February 2), the 2nd Chinese month (March 5 - April 3), the 3rd Chinese month (April 4 - May 4), and the 5th Chinese month (June 5 - July 6). Increase your safety and pay more attention to the health of the people in the house. Be careful of juniors or subordinates quarreling with neighbors. Be careful of valuables being damaged or lost, and danger from criminals. As for relatives, things are good. You will find friends who give good advice and help. There will be opportunities to travel together, relax, organize merit-making activities volunteer to help victims, or do public services.

Love

This year, young people will be loved and supported by adults. Therefore, they should behave well and be humble so that those they meet will feel love and compassion for them and will be the center of love for everyone in the house. For older people, they should behave appropriately and be a pillars for those who are younger so that their children and grandchildren will respect them. They should also not hang out at entertainment venues or indecent places because this may cause problems that will make them lose their respect. They should control their emotions in any action to nip them in the bud so that they do not get involved in unsolvable problems later on. Most importantly, they should not be picky with people around them because their spouses and close friends still love and care for them as usual. This year, they will have the opportunity to take their family members to visit distant relatives or take their lover on a vacation to reminisce about their love from their youth. But you should be careful during the months when your love life is likely to have conflicts, which are the 12th Chinese month (January 5 – February 2), the 2nd Chinese month (March 5 – April 3), the 3rd Chinese month (April 4 – May 4), and the 5th Chinese month (June 5 – July 6).

Health

For young people, even though they are young and healthy for their age, they should be careful of diseases related to the digestive system, allergies, and infectious diseases. Be careful of accidents from riding motorcycles and do not take the car out on the main road. As for senior people, they must be especially careful about their health because this year their body is not strong.

They must be strict about their diet, and be careful of intestinal diseases, diabetes, abnormal blood pressure and body aches, neck pain, back pain, and knee pain. When walking, be careful of dizziness which may cause slipping and falling because the horoscope house is plagued by evil stars. If you feel or feel anything unusual in your body, see a doctor for diagnosis and treatment.

In particular, the months when you need to take close care of your health are the 12th Chinese month (January 5 - February 2), the 2nd Chinese month (March 5 - April 3), the 3rd Chinese month (April 4 - May 4) and the 5th Chinese month (June 5 - July 6). Be careful and if you get sick, seek treatment immediately. Be careful of dangers during mourning.

Year of the GOAT (Water) | (1967)

"The Lost Goat" is a person born in the year of the GOAT at the age of 58 years (1967)

Overview

The person born in the year of the Goat, age 58, although this year the family's horoscope is smooth and bright, there will be auspicious energy visiting the house. Children will have good news. There will be happy things in the house. There is an opportunity to buy expensive property. Businesses will have new channels to open to prosperity. But during the year, the person born must be careful of various problems. Therefore, to eliminate bad luck and strengthen the horoscope of the auspicious star that comes to help, you should strengthen your charisma by practicing Dhamma, making merit, and donating to the underprivileged. Do not be careless in any work activities this year. You should always think carefully before doing anything. However, during the year, there will be a group of bad stars that will disturb the horoscope house, which will have a direct effect on health, illness, accidents, and loss of property. Therefore, this year is not suitable for investing in high-risk projects or projects in that you do not have enough knowledge or expertise because you have a chance of losing money from things that are beyond expectations. Therefore, when investing or joining a joint venture this year, you should be especially careful. Be careful of accounting fraud, be careful of lack of liquidity of working capital, and be careful of being tricked by others using fake documents to make various transactions.

In addition, you must be careful of being injured or attacked or sick with illnesses that threaten you, especially diabetes, high blood pressure, gastritis, stomach problems, problems of arguments, and problems of rifts in married life. You should be careful of your irritability which tends to take out your bad temper on others. It will cause people around you to run away. This year, you should start by taking care of your physical health to be strong. Take care of your mental health to be strong and comfortable. When you are not stressed, you can control your emotions and not make enemies or cause others to hate you. You should also try to avoid taking out your bad temper on others.

Career and Business

Even though this year your career and business direction will face storms, amidst the obstacles you will find someone to help you, making your work and business overall positive. However, you should still find an heir to take over your work. Even though you still have 100% energy to work today, looking for a replacement is not important. However, finding a replacement in advance will give you time to pass on the work more correctly. In particular, the months when your work will change for the better are the 6th Chinese month (July 7 – August 6), the 7th Chinese month (August 7 – September 6), the 9th Chinese month (October 8 – November 6), and the 10th Chinese month (November 7 – December 6). At this time, finding an heir to take care of your investments, both inside and outside the business, is expected to yield satisfactory returns and have the desired results. But you should be careful during the months when your work will face problems, namely the 12th Chinese month (January 5 - February 2), the 2nd Chinese month (March 5 - April 3), the 3rd Chinese month (April 4 - May 4), and the 5th Chinese month (June 5 - July 6). Investing at this time is not suitable because there is a chance of being deceived. Also, be careful of ill-wishers who invite you to invest more. You may experience losses. In addition, you should take good care of personnel management in your organization because there is a chance of conflicts that could lead to widespread damage. When making any contracts related to work, do not fall for flattery without checking the facts. It will be the cause of loss of property and loss.

Financial

This year's financial horoscope is a mix of good and bad. You should be careful of unexpected current expenses that may drain your money from the system. Also, do not be greedy for a small sum of money, which may cause you to lose a large sum of money. You should save unnecessary expenses to keep as reserves that can be used in emergencies. You should also allocate your investments correctly because if you enter the wrong market at the wrong time, you may suffer losses. This is especially true during the months when your finances are low: the 12th Chinese month (January 5 - February 2), the 2nd Chinese month (March 5 - April 3), the 3rd Chinese month (April 4 - May 4), and the 5th Chinese month (June 5 - July 6). During these periods, you should not lend money to others or guarantee anyone. You should not gamble or invest in risky and illegal businesses. Joint ventures with others or investing in securities should be avoided at this time so as not to cause any losses. The months when your finances will flow smoothly are the 6th Chinese month (7 July – 6 August), the 7th Chinese month (7 August – 6 September), the 9th Chinese month (8 October – 6 November) and the 10th Chinese month (7 November – 6 December).

Family

Even though this year there will be auspicious events and good things happening in your home, you should be careful of the influence of evil stars that may cause jealousy among acquaintances, which may cause harm to family members. In particular, the unstable months are the 12th Chinese month (January 5 – February 2), the 2nd Chinese month (March 5 – April 3), the 3rd Chinese month (April 4 – May 4), and the 5th Chinese month (June 5 – July 6), in which you must be especially careful. You should not get involved in internal matters or disputes between relatives. Be careful of accidents in your home and paying for medical expenses for close people. Be careful of people in your home being tricked into getting involved in lawsuits. In addition, be careful of falling victim to scammers and may suffer from mourning for an elder relative.

Love

This year, the beginning and end of the year will be smooth, but in the middle of the year, there will be problems with arguments. You will have quarrels and disagreements with your partner. Be careful not to fall for children because you will be tricked by children. Therefore, to reduce the problem of misunderstanding between you and your lover, you should be stable, think before you act, and always be mindful, then everything will pass. In addition, be careful of mood swings from menopause. It will make you irritable and may cause arguments easily, especially during the 12th Chinese month (January 5 - February 2), the 2nd Chinese month (March 5 - April 3), the 3rd Chinese month (April 4 - May 4), and the 5th Chinese month (June 5 - July 6). When going to a party, be careful that the big family will misunderstand. You should not get involved in other people's family matters. Be careful that your children do not show respect. It is best not to get involved in children's matters. Be careful of going to entertainment venues that may cause you to catch a disease.

Health

Due to the influence of the inauspicious stars, your health is not good. Therefore, you must be careful of silent diseases that will appear and make you sick. You should find time to get enough rest and try to reduce and quit all vices such as e-cigarettes, alcohol, and others because they all affect your health. In addition, you should be careful of abnormal blood pressure, shortness of breath, heart disease, and symptoms of inadequate blood flow to the brain, causing fainting. Therefore, what can help is to get enough sleep, find time to exercise, and see a doctor immediately if you feel that something is wrong, especially during the 12th Chinese month (January 5 - February 2), the 2nd Chinese month (March 5 - April 3), the 3rd Chinese month (April 4 - May 4), and the 5th Chinese month (June 5 - July 6), when the person should be strict about eating and drinking to be hygienic, control sugar, saltiness, and avoid foods high in fat. Be careful of old and new illnesses that will come calling, and be more careful of accidents both while working and traveling.

Year of the GOAT (Fire) | (1979)

" The Goats in the Pasture" is a person born in the year of the GOAT at the age of 46 years (1979)

Overview

The horoscope of the Goat in this age group, in terms of goodness, this year is considered another auspicious year. Your diligence will not be in vain. Your career will progress. A business will expand. External investment, both in terms of stocks and gold purchases, will have a good direction. There will be an opportunity to buy the right thing at the right time and sell it at a satisfactory price. Or if you buy and keep it, you will receive dividends as desired. But during the year, there will be bad stars visiting, namely "Star Kwang So" (Star of Chains) and "Star Tiang Kao" (Star of Blue Dog). It will have a significant effect on carelessness and lack of caution in investments. You will find that your debtor's account is in bad debt. You may also experience economic fluctuations or market changes that are beyond your control. This will be a major cause of your financial illiquidity. You should also be careful of arguments within the home. You will also find bad people looking for trouble. You cannot be careless or neglect health problems, both illnesses and injuries and bleeding from accidents, which may occur while working and while traveling. Therefore, you should be careful for your safety.

Career and Business
This year, for civil servants or government officials, there will be an opportunity to adjust to a better position. However, for those who work for a salary, be careful of subordinates

causing trouble and damage. For those who do business, you should visit your customers often. When releasing accounts, be careful not to just focus on increasing sales.

Especially during the months when your work will encounter problems, chaos, and obstacles, namely the 12th Chinese month (January 5 - February 2), the 2nd Chinese month (March 5 - April 3), the 3rd Chinese month (April 4 - May 4), and the 5th Chinese month (June 5 - July 6), be careful of finding a lost debtor account. When making employment contracts or hiring work, do not make decisions based on impulse or being challenged or provoked. Every activity should be considered clearly and thoroughly checked before doing it, otherwise, mistakes and damage will occur.

In addition, you should be careful of human resource management problems. Do not make hasty decisions in any way and be careful to control your emotions. Try not to show your dissatisfaction openly. Even if you are challenged or ridiculed, you must try to control your temper. Use reason and show your sincerity. The months in which your work and business will have a better direction are the 6th Chinese month (July 7 – August 6), the 7th Chinese month (August 7 – September 6), the 9th Chinese month (October 8 – November 6), and the 10th Chinese month (November 7 – December 6).

Financial

This year, even though there will be a lot of direct cash flow from salary or sales, including windfalls, due to the influence of evil stars, there will often be unexpected losses of large sums of money. Therefore, you should be especially careful during the 12th Chinese month (January 5th – February 2nd), the 2nd Chinese month (March 5th – April 3rd), the 3rd Chinese month (April 4th – May 4th), and the 5th Chinese month (June 5th – July 6th) when you are prohibited from lending money to or guaranteeing anyone with close friends. You are prohibited from gambling or taking risks. You are prohibited from getting involved in illegal or immoral businesses. You are prohibited from greedy for wealth that does not belong to you. You must also be careful of losing wealth from subordinates or subordinates. Throughout the year, you should cut out unnecessary expenses and manage your income and expenses carefully. The months when your finances will flow smoothly are the 6th Chinese month (July 7 – August 6), the 7th Chinese month (August 7 – September 6), the 9th Chinese month (October 8 – November 6), and the 10th Chinese month (November 7 – December 6).

Family

This year, the family will lack peace due to the influence of the evil stars. The person may resolve the problem by buying expensive things that they have liked since the beginning of the year. This is considered a solution to the problem of losing money. Also, be careful of people in the house arguing with neighbors until it becomes a grudge that wants to settle the score, causing a lack of peace for both parties. Especially during the months when the family will experience problems and conflicts, namely the 12th Chinese month (January 5 - February 2), the 2nd Chinese month (March 5 - April 3), the 3rd Chinese month (April 4 - May 4), and the 5th Chinese month (June 5 - July 6). Be extra careful, especially about illnesses of family members. Using the tools and equipment of family members and accidents will cause bloodshed. Be careful of lawsuits with others. Therefore, this year, you should not get involved if your friends have disputes. Be careful of getting involved in lawsuits and encountering difficulties. You may also be hated and targeted for revenge. Be careful of falling victim to scammers.

Love
This year, the love of this person will not be smooth. It is easy for storms to strike each other. You should be careful to control your emotions and not let them explode easily. Otherwise, the path will only lead to breakups. Especially during the months when your love is fragile and problems can easily occur, namely the 12th Chinese month (January 5 - February 2), the 2nd Chinese month (March 5 - April 3),

the 3rd Chinese month (April 4 - May 4), and the 5th Chinese month (June 5 - July 6). Be careful not to get involved in other people's family problems. Be careful of a third party who may come close to you and cause misunderstandings. Or you should control your temper. Be careful of people who pretend to be close during this period. If you let yourself slip, it will cause endless problems. In addition, avoid hanging out at entertainment venues. Be careful of catching diseases.

Health

This year, the health of the person is not very strong because of the influence of the evil stars that are orbiting and directly targeting the health base. Therefore, you should be careful of injuries and blood from sharp objects, as well as dangers from accidents and illnesses. Especially during the months when health problems will occur, which are the 12th Chinese month (January 5 - February 2), the 2nd Chinese month (March 5 - April 3), the 3rd Chinese month (April 4 - May 4), and the 5th Chinese month (June 5 - July 6). Be careful of dizziness and fainting. If you drink alcohol or have a hangover, you should not drive or work with machinery because it may cause an accident. You should also be careful when using the road. In addition, you should avoid visiting sick patients at night and should find time to exercise regularly, get enough sleep, and always take care of your drinking and eating habits to have good immunity.

Year of the GOAT (Earth) | (1991)

"The lucky goat" is a person born in the year of the GOAT at the age of 34 years (1991)

Overview

For the Goat horoscope in this age group, this year is another good time because during the year you will find a patron. Your career will progress. Your business will expand. Therefore, the important thing to do this year is to be humble and have good human relations. You should approach your elders often and maintain good relationships with friends and business partners. In addition, you should promote yourself by increasing new skills and knowledge that are up to date with the situation. Do not stop adding knowledge to yourself to adapt to the changes.

However, during the year, the horoscope house is harassed by a group of bad stars. The influence of this group of stars will harm both you and your family. It will cause various problems such as accidents, arguments, and legal problems. Therefore, you should be more careful. The solution must be based on the cause. For accidents, you should not be careless in your life and driving.

Avoid arguing. If there is a lawsuit, you should solve it by following the law. Do business that is a good profession. Respect the rights of others, be humble, have good manners, have good human relations skills, and know how to be diligent, safe, and patient. It will give you a bright future and allow you to reach your goal. There is another thing you should be careful about this year: choosing friends is important and being careful. Trusting your friends too much, be careful that you will end up being disheartened.

Career and Business

The career and business of this age group may not be extremely prosperous, but it is not low either. This is because when facing problems this year, you will find a patron to help you. There is a chance to receive support from your boss and colleagues. Therefore, please be diligent in your work. Your work will impress your elders. If you have your own business or do business, this year, whether your sales will be good or bad depends on your frequent visits to customers and your interactions with people you have to deal with consistently. This will allow you to expand your sales to their fullest potential. This is an opportunity to buy new businesses expand branches or invest more. In particular, the months when your work and trade will change in a better direction are the 6th Chinese month (July 7 – August 6), the 7th Chinese month (August 7 – September 6), the 9th Chinese month (October 8 – November 6), and the 10th Chinese month (November 7–

December 6). However, you should be careful during the months when your work will encounter problems, including the 12th Chinese month (January 5 – February 2), the 2nd Chinese month (March 5– April 3), the 3rd Chinese month (April 4 – May 4), and the 5th Chinese month (June 5 – July 6). During the aforementioned periods, you should not be hasty in working, make hasty decisions, or rush to conclusions because mistakes or damage may occur. When making an employment contract or being hired, you should carefully check the details of the contract before deciding to sign it. You should also not invest in new things or increase your investment. You should also be careful of subordinates causing you trouble.

Financial

This year, the money flow will be good because you will have the opportunity to expand your business. Moreover, your investment will have good returns, resulting in more income and the opportunity to gain fortune from gambling. The months when you will have financial fortune are the 6th Chinese month (July 7 – August 6), the 7th Chinese month (August 7 – September 6), the 9th Chinese month (October 8 – November 6), and the 10th Chinese month (November 7 – December 6). However, even though this year your income will be high, there will be unexpectedly large expenses that will overtake your income. If you know how to save, you will have some left over. However, if you are not careful, you may end up in a deep deficit. Especially during the 12th Chinese month (January 5- February 2), 2nd Chinese month (March 5 - April 3), 3rd Chinese month (April 4 - May 4), and 5th Chinese month (June 5 - July 6) when it is forbidden to lend money to others and be a guarantor for anyone. Gambling and taking risks are forbidden. You should not invest in businesses that are at risk of breaking the law or being immoral. Take good care of the liquidity in the system, otherwise, you may experience a financial crisis.

Family
This year, the family is likely to encounter good fortune and evil fortune. Even though the

auspicious stars are supporting it, there will be evil stars blocking it. Therefore, the person should be careful, especially regarding health and safety issues of the people in the house, including arguments and conflicts, and beware of mourning for the elders. In particular, during the months when there will be problems and chaos in your family, namely the 12th Chinese month (January 5 – February 2), the 2nd Chinese month (March 5 – April 3), the 3rd Chinese month (April 4 – May 4), and the 5th Chinese month (June 5 – July 6), you must increase your inspection and be careful about safety in your home, whether it is the roof, ceiling, electrical appliances, or anything that is attached in high places. If anything is damaged, it should be replaced or repaired so that it is still usable. Try to reduce the factors that will cause arguments among people in the house. Be careful of the younger neighbors who come to cause trouble, and be careful of falling victim to scammers. In addition, you should be able to analyze and distinguish your friends and see who is hiding something suspicious, which will help a bit.

Love

This year, love is due to the power of the chrysanthemum (the power of charm and deceit) and the demon star that is orbiting to threaten and focus on you. Your love is therefore unstable. Your mind is often wavering. In addition, there is often a third party that is constantly nagging and has the same opinion. It is like the old love has run out of promotion. Everything seems to be stuck and problematic. You should be careful during the months when your love is quite fragile and arguments can easily occur, namely the 12th Chinese month (January 5 - February 2), the 2nd Chinese month (March 5 - April 3), the 3rd Chinese month (April 4 - May 4), and the 5th Chinese month (June 5 - July 6). Be careful not to get involved in other people's families and be careful with words that will hurt your partner. Avoid going to entertainment venues and places of vice because there will be endless dangers and troubles.

Health

This year, health is moderate. There will be some minor illnesses, but they will be cured and not serious. However, due to the power of the Peach Blossom threatening the horoscope, the person will likely suffer from illnesses related to love and the sharp blood star that is staring at them, which will result in injuries, bloodshed, and other illnesses that will annoy. The months that you need to take close care of your health are the 12th Chinese month (January 5 - February 2), the 2nd Chinese month (March 5 - April 3), the 3rd Chinese month (April 4 - May 4), and the 5th Chinese month (June 5 - July 6). Do not rush any activities or work because a single mistake can mean a major disaster. Therefore, to be on the safe side, even if you are a little late, you will arrive home safely. Be careful of illnesses from traveling.

Chinese Astrology Horoscope for Each Month

Month 12 in the Dragon Year (5 Jan 25 - 2 Feb 25)
The horoscope of those born in the year of the Goat has moved to the destructive line this month. In addition, there are groups of evil stars orbiting to disturb the horoscope house. The important thing you should be careful of is ill-wishers who are secretly looking for ways to harm and harass you, waiting for the right moment to make a mistake and attack you. Therefore, if you are thinking of doing any work or planning anything, you must be more careful and thorough in everything. Also, always prepare a backup plan for unexpected unexpected events. What you should do this month is to do good but not stand out or it will be a threat. Whether it is words, behavior, gestures, or all-around interpersonal skills, you must be balanced. You should also be humble and gentle with the wind, rather than being a hard pine tree that is hard to break. This will help you escape disaster. In addition, you should closely check your accounting system and manage your working capital. Do not be too bold in doing anything beyond your ability. It

will only drag down your liquidity and make you unable to make ends meet. In terms of work and business, there will be storms during this period. Be careful of conflicts among people in the organization. Be careful of unexpected incidents that will affect your main job. However, you should do your best in your job, and be neutral and fair in managing people at work. Also, during this period, you must be careful when signing any contracts related to work or trade, as you may be deceived or disadvantaged. You must be careful. Investments this month are not good.

For your finances, you will lose money this month. Therefore, you should spend sparingly. You should not gamble or take risks. You should not be greedy for the benefit of others.

In terms of family, it is moderate. Find time to do activities together to increase your relationship.

Love is good. You will meet someone of the opposite sex who you like and your love will be reciprocated. However, if you seek temporary love from an entertainment venue, you may encounter illnesses in return.

In terms of health, it is moderate. You should exercise regularly and eat healthy food.

Support Days: 2 Jan., 6 Jan., 10 Jan., 14 Jan., 18 Jan., 22 Jan., 26 Jan., 30 Jan.
Lucky Days: 1 Jan., 13 Jan., 25 Jan.
Misfortune Days: 8 Jan., 20 Jan.
Bad Days: 5 Jan., 7 Jan., 17 Jan., 19 Jan., 29 Jan., 31 Jan.

Month 1 in the Snake Year (3 Feb 25 - 4 Mar 25)
This month, your horoscope is moving towards a partnership, helping to promote many things that have been stuck and stalled to be able to continue smoothly. In terms of work, you will have the opportunity to create work that will lead to progress. Businesses will encounter good opportunities to make money. Therefore, what you should do on this occasion is to be more diligent and persistent in your work because the more you do, the more you will

receive. Create work that will expand sales and income. You should also push forward various projects that you have planned to become tangible as soon as possible under a smooth period without obstacles.

This month's financial horoscope is good. There will be money flowing in from two sources: direct from your regular salary or sales from products or services. As for special money from special jobs, brokerage fees, or money from good fortune, there will be an inflow. However, you must know how to save for the month when your finances are low. As for investments in various areas during this period, you will receive good returns in return.

As for your family horoscope, it is peaceful, and auspicious power is visiting you. You are likely to receive good news about the success of people in your home or within your family, there is a possibility of organizing any auspicious work. There may be new members or you may have the opportunity to move into a new house. As for your relatives and friends, they will support and help you very well.

In terms of health, it is in a good condition. Even though there are minor illnesses, it is because the weather is not severe. However, this month, you cannot be careless or complacent about accidents while traveling near or far.

As for sweet love, this is another month when the opposite sex is interested in being close.

Support Days: 3 Feb., 7 Feb., 11 Feb., 15 Feb., 19 Feb., 23 Feb., 27 Feb.
Lucky Days: 6 Feb., 18 Feb.
Misfortune Days: 1 Feb., 13 Feb., 25 Feb.
Bad Days: 10 Feb., 12 Feb., 22 Feb., 24 Feb.

Month 2 in the Snake Year (5 Mar 25 - 3 Apr 25)

This month, your horoscope will encounter a big wave that will affect your work and management. For those who work regularly, your work will have obstacles. You will encounter conflicts and chaos among people that will cause you headaches. For those who do business, you will encounter enemies and competitors who will try to block and obstruct you. You will have to use every strategy to compete for market share and customer base.

In terms of work, be careful of subordinates who will cause problems that you will have to solve. In addition, negotiations and agreements regarding work must be meticulous. You cannot be hasty in your work because mistakes can easily occur. As for starting a new job, investing, or entering into a joint venture, this month is not a suitable opportunity. What you should do this month is to manage your personnel to reduce conflicts. You must also be careful not to be the one causing conflicts yourself and not use emotions in your work. Always build and strengthen good relationships with people around you so that work flows smoothly. For the work that you are assigned, you must understand it clearly before doing it. Know how to adjust and change to keep up with external situations and you will be able to overcome various obstacles.

This month, your financial horoscope will encounter storms. Therefore, you should not lend money to anyone or accept guarantees. Gambling and taking risks are prohibited. You should save money and take good care of your cash flow.

Your family will be peaceful. In terms of health, be careful of stomach diseases, intestinal diseases, and food poisoning. Beware of accidents at home and while traveling, as they may cause injury. For relatives and friends, during this time, beware of two-faced friends. What they do to your face will cause you damage and trouble behind your back. In terms of love, do not be gullible and listen to gossip. Do not interfere in other people's family matters. Beware of arguments. Avoid going to entertainment venues, as you may catch a disease as a bonus.

Support Days: 3 Mar, 7 Mar., 11 Mar., 15 Mar., 19 Mar., 23 Mar., 27 Mar., 31 Mar.
Lucky Days: 2 Mar, 14 Mar., 26 Mar.
Misfortune Days: 9 Mar, 21 Mar.
Bad Days: 6 Mar, 8 Mar., 18 Mar., 20 Mar., 30 Mar.

Month 3 in the Snake Year (4 Apr 25 - 4 May 25)
This month, your life path has moved to a deadly line, so there will be a story of overlapping obstacles that are both chaotic and confusing. If you don't manage it well, you might lose the good relationships you've built. What you should do this month is to take care of your work and responsibilities to the fullest extent, and avoid problems with people around you, in other words, help yourself survive first before helping and giving advice to others. In terms of conflicts, you must remain neutral, not clearly show that you are taking sides, and should always be humble and respectful. If there is a problem in your work, fix it

immediately. Do not leave it for too long until it is difficult to recover. You should also be careful of accidents both during work and travel.

This month's financial horoscope is not good, with little income and high expenses. Be careful of unexpected current expenses and be careful of debtors who have bad debt accounts. Do not gamble or take risks. Do not invest in illegal businesses because you might face prison.

In terms of work, be careful of personnel management, as conflicts may arise. You must also be careful of accounting fraud and mistakes during work. Investments and joint ventures should be postponed during this period.

As for your family, be careful of the safety of your family members, and be careful of arguments between family members and falling victim to scammers. But for relatives and friends, you may have to keep your distance during this period because it will bring trouble.

For health this month, you will be strong, but you must be careful of injuries from unexpected accidents and being hit by stray bullets from arguments or you may have to share responsibility for a friend's lawsuit.

For love, if there are obstacles or problems, you will receive good help from your lover. It is a good time for singles to open their hearts and move forward to ask for love.

Support Days: 4 Apr., 8 Apr., 12 Apr., 16 Apr., 20 Apr., 24 Apr., 28 Apr.
Lucky Days: 7 Apr., 19 Apr.
Misfortune Days: 2 Apr., 14 Apr., 26 Apr.
Bad Days: 1 Apr., 11 Apr., 13 Apr., 23 Apr., 25 Apr.

Month 4 in the Snake Year (5 May 25 - 4 Jun 25)
This month, your horoscope is moving in a better direction, but the big problems that are causing you worry have not disappeared. Coupled with your rather unstable mind, there is only restlessness and anxiety, making you unable to see through the problems, which often causes you to miss good opportunities. Therefore, what you should do this month is to examine yourself. What are your weaknesses? What are your strengths? What are your opportunities? What are you still lacking? So that you can fix what you lack, fill in new skills in the missing parts, study the work under your responsibility in-depth, research the market, keep up with the changing preferences of consumers, and keep up with the surrounding situation that changes all the time. Most importantly, you must be decisive. You must quickly resolve any problems or obstacles that you have because your horoscope has patrons. However, because your mind is still hesitant, in terms of work and investment, if you consider carefully and thoroughly, you should not hesitate. You can do it.

This month, your financial horoscope is moderate to low. Gambling should not be your main priority. If you play for fun with a limited budget, it is better than being greedy and losing your fortune. In addition, do not be careless at all. You must allocate your income into parts for saving and investing.

Your career horoscope is the time to prepare for a big job. For those who are in business, this is the time to prepare a budget to buy to open the market and expand new channels again. You should prepare to accumulate factors and manpower.

Within the family, this month is peaceful. There are no bad things to worry about. But health is moderate. Old diseases, even if you feel better, should be treated continuously because they may flare up and become bigger than before later. You should also take care of your hygiene in terms of living and eating. Relatives and friends are good. You will receive help from these people.

Love horoscope is the time for drinking honeymoon. Singles, the relationship will progress well. For those with families, your partner is attentive and caring. This is a good time to travel and relax for a second or third honeymoon.

Support Days: 2 May., 6 May., 10 May., 14 May., 18 May., 22 May., 26 May., 30 May.
Lucky Days: 1 May., 13 May., 25 May.
Misfortune Days: 8 May., 20 May.
Bad Days: 5 May, 7 May, 17 May., 19 May., 29 May., 31 May.

Month 5 in the Snake Year (5 Jun 25 - 6 Jul 25)
This month, your horoscope has moved in a negative direction. The direction of your horoscope that is moving forward has decreased, causing your work and business to face unexpected obstacles again. You have to constantly solve daily problems with subordinates or subordinates causing trouble and damage. You also have to be careful about embezzlement in accounting and any

document and contract transactions. During this time, you have to be careful not to be tricked or put at a disadvantage. Therefore, you should look carefully and carefully before doing anything. In terms of management, you have to be very careful about conflicts between people. The most important thing this month is to keep your wits about you and not be too stressed. Think slowly and encourage yourself. Only a stable mind can you get through the crisis. The most important thing you should do during this time is to not rush to show yourself when you encounter something. This time, you may encounter something good and have the right to suffer instead of others. Also, this month, making friends is not knowing their faces. Be careful of sweet talkers who hide knives behind their backs. Investments or collaborations are not good during this time.

Your financial horoscope this month is in a state of losing money. Emergency expenses will appear. When your income is low and your expenses are high, you should save more. This month, you should avoid gambling and taking risks and do not lend money or invest in businesses that are likely to be illegal. Do not be greedy and hope for other people's benefits. Also, be careful of bad debts from customers who are still in the account, which will lead to bad debts that affect liquidity.

For the family horoscope, there is a bad star in focus, so you should be careful of safety and pay attention to the health of the people in the house. Also, be careful of mourning for the elderly relatives. Be careful of valuables being damaged or lost, and be careful of falling victim to fraud.

As for love, there is a chance of arguments. Therefore, you should not go to entertainment venues or get involved in other people's married lives. Also, be careful of a third party interfering.

In terms of health, during this period, be careful of insomnia. Also, while working or driving, be careful of injuries from accidents.

Support Days: 3 Jun., 7 Jun., 11 Jun., 15 Jun., 19 Jun., 23 Jun., 27 Jun.
Lucky Days: 6 Jun., 18 Jun., 30 Jun.
Misfortune Days: 1 Jun., 13 Jun., 25 Jun.
Bad Days: 10 Jun., 12 Jun., 22 Jun., 24 Jun.

Month 6 in the Snake Year (7 Jul 25 - 6 Aug 25)
This month, your life path will soar again. This is another good period for your business expansion plan. You don't have to think about it again. You can start doing it right away. In addition, you have a sponsor to help and support you. Therefore, be determined and diligent. Go ahead and do it. Don't miss out on opportunities. The important thing this month is that you have to wake up early and work harder than others. Otherwise, your opportunities and money may be snatched away by your competitors.

Your financial horoscope this month is good. You will get regular money from sales, salary, and special money from special jobs. However, your windfall luck is dark. Therefore, you should avoid it so that you don't get hurt. You should also avoid risky investments this month.

In terms of work, you will find a path of progress. Your business will flourish. However, you will have to fill up your courage, new skills, and diligence to be successful.

However, starting a new job, entering into a joint venture, and investing in various projects will cause ill-wishers to come and deceive you, causing damage and suffering.

Your family horoscope is smooth. Your house has auspicious energy. There will be good news about success or another auspicious event. However, you have to be careful about your relatives and friends because some friends are trying to stab you in the back.

As for your love horoscope, this month is sweet and full of happiness. But you still have to pay attention and always add sweetness to your married life. Don't neglect the time you should have for your family. Instead, you should prioritize and divide your work and love time appropriately.

For those who are still single, if the person you are dating loves you and hopes to marry you, please hurry up and negotiate. Otherwise, you may be cut off by a good person and you may lose your lover.

In terms of health, you are still healthy and strong. There is nothing to worry about.

Support Days: 1 Jul., 5 Jul., 9 Jul., 13 Jul., 17 Jul., 21 Jul., 25 Jul., 29 Jul.
Lucky Days: 12 Jul., 24 Jul.
Misfortune Days: 7 Jul., 19 Jul., 31 Jul.
Bad Days: 4 Jul., 6 Jul.,16 Jul., 18 Jul., 28 Jul., 30 Jul.

Month 7 in the Snake Year (7 Aug 25 - 6 Sep 25)

This month, your horoscope, even though the auspicious stars are shining, causing many things to change for the better, is still not over the storm. Work and business still have obstacles. There are also conflicts between people in the organization that cannot be resolved and reconciled. Therefore, this month, you should be careful that starting a good atmosphere at work must start with your patience, to endure various frictions from things around you that are often changing.

This month, your finances will fall and you will lose money. You will have unexpected expenses. Therefore, you should not gamble and take risks, and do not be greedy because it will cause more damage. It is better to save as much as possible.

For work this month, be careful of problems with customers or people you interact with often. You should take good care of them so that they do not become problems later. In terms of family, you will find someone to help you, be a tonic for your heart, and be a consultant. Things that are troubling you and causing you suffering will improve. In terms of investment, if you want to do it, you should consult an experienced elder, otherwise you will encounter problems later.

In terms of love, it is not smooth. Those who have a lover or partner should be patient. Do not let your emotions or selfishness control you because no one can please you in every way, not even yourself. Therefore, you must be flexible and adapt. As for those who are single, make time to be close to each other. Water dripping on the rock every day will erode the rock, so you have to keep trying.

Health-wise, be careful of allergies, liver disease, stomach disease, and intestinal disease, control your alcohol consumption, and be careful of accidents both at work and while traveling.

Support Days: 2 Aug., 6 Aug., 10 Aug., 14 Aug., 18 Aug., 22 Aug., 26 Aug., 30 Aug.
Lucky Days: 5 Aug., 17 Aug., 29 Aug.
Misfortune Days: 12 Aug., 24 Aug.
Bad Days: 9 Aug., 11 Aug., 21 Aug., 23 Aug.

Month 8 in the Snake Year (7 Sep 25 - 7 Oct 25)

Since this month's life path is moving to meet the bad stars, your destiny will decline and fall, causing your work and business to encounter obstacles. There will often be competitors trying to snatch your place. In addition, the influence of the stars will often affect accidents or unexpected unusual events, including illnesses. Therefore, you must be more careful in all activities. Most importantly, you must be calm, not rash and greedy because it may cause damage and loss of property. The important thing you should do this month is to adhere to the principle of saving and moderation, and take good care of your business's liquidity and working capital. Be careful of leakage points. If you encounter any problems, do not be forthright. Also, be careful about drinking.

Be careful when alcohol enters your mouth because it will make you speak unpleasantly to others. It may cause your mouth to turn red.

In terms of fortune and finance, this month you will be in a position to lose property. Therefore, do not lend money to others or be a guarantor.

You should not gamble, take risks, invest illegally, or infringe on others' copyrights because you may be imprisoned for dividends. You should also refrain from investing in stocks and other investments for the time being.

In terms of work, you will encounter storms. You should maintain good relationships with people around you and with customers you have to contact regularly. Do not neglect them at all.

Your family's fortune is not smooth. Because the sinful planets are in orbit this month, you must be careful of people in the house getting injured from accidents and there may be danger of mourning for the elders.

In terms of health, you have a chance of getting sick from food poisoning and must be careful of injuries from accidents while traveling.

As for love, do not get involved in matters that are not yours because it will lead to arguments.

Support Days: 3 Sep, 7 Sep., 11 Sep, 15 Sep, 19 Sep., 23 Sep., 27 Sep.
Lucky Days: 10 Sep, 22 Sep.
Misfortune Days: 5 Sep, 17 Sep., 29 Sep
Bad Days: 2 Sep, 4 Sep., 14 Sep, 16 Sep, 26 Sep., 28 Sep

Month 9 in the Snake Year (8 Oct 25 - 6 Nov 25)
This month, your fortune will gradually improve. Your career and business will find a sponsor. It is like a bird that is lucky and can fly far away. Therefore, what you should do this month is to not forget to build good relationships at both the top and bottom levels because big projects cannot be completed by yourself. You need cooperation and help from all parties.

Your financial fortune this month is good. If you work hard, you will receive a lot of money. There will be income flowing in from many sources according to what you have invested and worked hard for. There will also be an opportunity to receive special money from luck. Some people who need capital may start saving money this month. For those who need extra income, you may go to study a vocational course to create opportunities for yourself. This month, you will be charming with your words. Therefore, you should build friendships and relationships with customers or those you have to do business with. This will help your work progress even further.

In terms of work and business, problems will arise due to communication. Therefore, you should not rush to a conclusion but should focus on communicating clearly. In addition, conflicts will linger like a shadow. You must dare to make decisions about pending problems to minimize the damage caused by the conclusion because letting it drag on will not make anything better. On the contrary, it will cause more damage. As for starting a new job, This month, you can choose to invest in joint ventures and get good returns.

This month, family horoscope, be careful of arguments in the house, including people inside fighting with outsiders. Avoid it by not interfering in other people's matters.

Love horoscope is good, there is a good time for auspicious work, whether it is asking for a proposal, getting engaged, getting married, or moving out.

In terms of health, if there is an illness, it can be easily treated, but you should not be careless. You still have to exercise every day and always eat healthy food.

Support Days: 1 Oct., 5 Oct., 9 Oct., 13 Oct., 17 Oct., 21 Oct., 25 Oct, 29 Oct.
Lucky Days: 4 Oct., 16 Oct., 28 Oct.
Misfortune Days: 11 Oct., 23 Oct.
Bad Days: 8 Oct., 10 Oct., 20 Oct., 22 Oct.

Month 10 in the Snake Year (7 Nov 25 - 6 Dec 25)
This month, your fate is moving smoothly. In addition, auspicious stars will appear, radiating auspicious energy. The power of patronage will come to help dissolve various inauspicious

energy. Therefore, if you have the opportunity, you should make merit and do good deeds. It will help relieve and reduce serious misfortunes to light. There are important things that you should do: When the sky opens up and allows you to do so, you should diligently follow your plans and put all your resources into it. Use your intelligence to the best of your ability. This opportunity will receive good feedback. In addition, you should be honest to defeat your competitors and make those you have to contact see your sincerity towards others.

For financial fortune, direct wealth will flow in sufficiently. Liquidity is still good, but you must be careful not to be overly generous. You should only spend when necessary. Otherwise, you will suffer later. Furthermore, there is only a small amount of windfall luck. Therefore, you must not be greedy. When you have it, you must know when to stop and when to stop.

As for your work, it will continue to progress, which may be because the problems have been solved. You will also find someone to help you solve problems. For various investments, this month will have a good future.

Your family horoscope is moderate, but you must be careful that the happy things that come in during this period will be just a castle in the air, causing you to be disappointed.

In terms of love, it is smooth. Your lover will be sweet to you, but please don't be too sweet. Most importantly, don't pick or smell flowers by the roadside, as they will be harmful in the long run. You should avoid them.

Health horoscope: Even though you may get sick, it won't be serious. Eat healthy food and exercise regularly.

Support Days: 2 Nov., 6 Nov., 10 Nov., 14 Nov., 18 Nov., 22 Nov., 26 Nov., 30 Nov.
Lucky Days: 9 Nov., 21 Nov.
Misfortune Days: 4 Nov., 16 Nov., 28 Nov.
Bad Days: 1 Nov., 3 Nov., 13 Nov., 15 Nov., 25 Nov., 27 Nov.

Month 11 in the Snake Year (7 Dec 25 - 4 Jan 26)

This month, your horoscope is still going strong from last month. The path is quite smooth. Obstacles that you used to have are resolved. What you should do now is to quickly create work and make sales. Also, you should always remember not to show off or show off your skills because it will be dangerous. In addition, you should know how to give what you should give to the person you should give it to. Second, behave in the right way, which will help you be mindful and have a good image. Third, be patient with anger and hardship. Fourth, be diligent. Fifth, analyze every aspect of your work to know it thoroughly. And lastly, be intelligent, which will help you turn the situation around, no matter how much of a storm there is.

This month, your financial horoscope is bright. Cash flow will continuously flow in both directions. There are still many positive investment channels, so it is a good opportunity for you to seize it.

In terms of work, even though there is damage, the results are still showing results. Therefore, you should pay more attention and be diligent. Sales and income will increase. Starting a new job, joining a joint venture, or investing in various projects during this period will have a useful return.

For families, this month, you will find auspicious wealth. This is another month where you are likely to receive good news from your family members.

As for love blossoming sweetly, there will be an opportunity to travel together to create understanding and add sweetness to each other.

As for health, this month is good. Pains in the body and various aches and pains are reduced.

Support Days: 4 Dec., 8 Dec., 12 Dec., 16 Dec., 20 Dec., 24 Dec., 28 Dec.

Lucky Days: 3 Dec., 15 Dec., 27 Dec.

Misfortune Days: 10 Dec., 22 Dec.

Bad Days: 7 Dec., 9 Dec., 19 Dec., 21 Dec., 31 Dec.

Amulet for The Year of the Goat

"The four guardian deities hold a magical umbrella."

Those born in the year of the Goat this year should set up and worship the sacred object "Lord Chatulokban Krong Romwiset" to enhance their destiny. Place it on your work desk or cash desk to ask for his power and authority to help promote your career and business to be smooth and progress, be wealthy have a peaceful and happy family, and be safe from disasters throughout the year.

In one chapter of the Advanced Feng Shui, it was mentioned that the deities who will come down to reside in the Mie Keng (House of Destiny) of the year are deities who can bring both good and bad fortune to the deities of that year. Therefore, worshiping to enhance your destiny with the deities who come down to reside in your birth year is considered to have the best results and have the most impact on you. This is to rely on the power of that deity to help protect you while your destiny is declining and having bad karma to alleviate it. At the same time, ask for his blessing to help your business and business go smoothly as desired, and bring glory and prosperity to you and your family.

Those born in the year of the Goat or Mie Keng (horoscope house) in the zodiac sign B, this year will be a year where everything is quite stuck and there is no luck. Projects and projects often encounter obstacles that prevent them from easily achieving their goals. This is because this year the horoscope is influenced by the evil star "Kuang Sao" (chain star), which spreads its influence and causes you to often have constant worries and worries. Although this year your work will encounter obstacles and there will often be problems with people that need to be resolved, what will help to reduce the severity is honesty and sincerity towards people and doing business honestly so that problems do not follow. During the year, you should be careful of the unevenness from the evil star "Buang Sing" (the planet of danger) that is orbiting to harass you, which will directly affect your health, illness, accidents, and loss of property, as well as being careful of scammers. Therefore, when starting a new job or investing this year, you must be very careful. Also, when traveling near or far, you should not be careless with accidents. There is a possibility of mourning for an elder relative. This year, the love situation will remain the same. However, common health problems are allergies and joint pain. Therefore, if you think of solving and dispelling the power of the evil star, You should establish and worship "Lord Chatulokbala Krongsamitesat" to break the destructive power of the inauspicious stars and promote the horoscope to be smooth and bright. Your career and business will flourish without obstacles and problems. Your health will be strong and free from illness and suffering throughout the year.

Lord "To Ung Tian Wong" (or Lord Vessuwan Maharach) is considered one of the "Shi Tian Wang" (Xi Tai Tian Wong) or the four Lord Chatulokbala who are the leaders of the Chatumaharajika heaven, which is the land of the gods that borders the human world. The four great gods act as the world guardians (protectors of the world) in the four major directions. They are responsible for maintaining peace and order to support the righteous people who are steadfast in morality in both the human and divine worlds. In addition, "Lord Chatulokbala" is considered a "God of Dharma" or "Hu Huab", which is the guardian of the Dharma or the guardian of Buddhism. He is also a god who protects and looks after various religious places and helps protect and maintain countries that believe in Buddhism. In particular, his main duty is "To Ung Thian Wong" (the great god who holds a magical umbrella) who was assigned by the Buddha to help take care of the wind and rain so that it falls in season so that the people can make a living smoothly. He is like a great god who helps people to have a prosperous and abundant life.

They live well and eat well without encountering hardship, poverty, and all kinds of suffering. However, people who receive wealth, money, and various kinds of help must be good and adhere to morality and virtue.

In addition, those born in the year of the Goat should wear a sacred pendant of "Lord Chatulokpala holding a magical umbrella" around their necks or carry it with them when traveling outside the home, whether near or far, so that the person will be filled with auspicious wealth and properties, have prosperity and progress in both business and trade and have a peaceful and happy family throughout the year, resulting in better and faster efficiency and effectiveness than before.

Good Direction: Northwest, Southwest, and East
Bad Direction: Northeast
Lucky Colors: Cream, Gold, Yellow, and Brown.
Lucky Times: 11.00 – 12.59, 13.00 – 14.59, 21.00 – 22.59.
Bad Times: 01.00 – 02.59, 19.00 – 20.59., 25.00 – 00.59

Good Luck For 2025

www.ingramcontent.com/pod-product-compliance
Lightning Source LLC
Chambersburg PA
CBHW051808130726

47987CB00003B/1164